MATLAB

SCRIPTING

&

FILE

PROCESSING

Daniel Okoh and Eric Nwokolo

Preface

This book is intended as an easy-to-use guide for persons interested in using MATLAB to develop programs which they can share, give or sell to others. Persons always working with bulks of data stored or saved in so many files will also find this book useful. The book illustrates, in simple manner, how to develop MATLAB programs (or scripts) which can be used by others in their own computers. It also explains how data or items contained in a file could be read into MATLAB, and how data from MATLAB can be written to files on the user's computer.

Daniel Okoh
NASRDA Center for Atmospheric Research, Kogi State University, Anyigba, Nigeria.
[okodan2003@gmail,com, +2348136094616]

Eric Nwokolo
Department of Electrical Engineering, University of Nigeria, Nsukka, Nigeria.
[nwokoloeric@yahoo.com, +2348064090637]

Table of Contents

Chapter One:

MATLAB SCRIPTING

Scripting in MATLAB is simply a way of writing MATLAB programs into a file that can be saved and used later on, or even copied to a different computer where it can also be used. This is a fantastic way of making programs reusable, and only on the click of a button.

In our introductory book 'Introduction to MATLAB', the programs were typed and ran directly on the command window [You may want to first read that book if you've never used MATLAB before]. Programs typed and ran directly on the command window fall short, in some usages, compared to ones written and saved to files (also called scripts). We only highlight the following two:

1. Scripting allows you to first type in your entire list of commands (can be up to hundreds or thousands of commands) and later run/execute them automatically in the sequence they were typed. In the real-world, utility programs are like this. But commands typed unto the command window can only be run manually, one at a time.

2. Scripting also allows you to have file which you can share, give or sell to others. They only need to copy it onto their computers and run/execute it from there without bothering to have an idea of what the commands in the file are. This is not possible with typing and running commands directly on the command window.

Without wasting time, we'll want to get started!

1.1 Starting a MATLAB Script

MATLAB Scripting is usually done on the MATLAB Editor, and to start/open the editor, we can either

a. go to File → New → Script, or

b. click the 'New Script' icon on the MATLAB toolbar

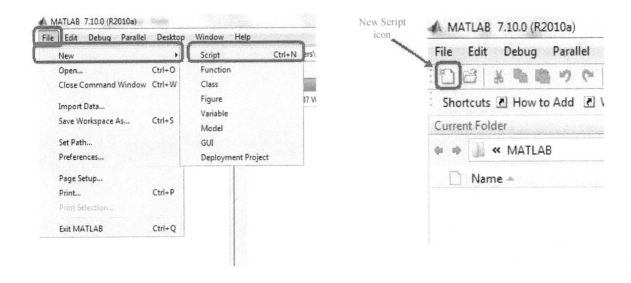

Once this is done, a new and empty script is opened as shown below

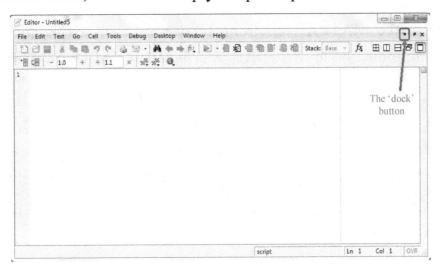

This scripting environment is also called the MATLAB Editor, and if it is your first time to do so, the editor usually opens on a separate window.

We can also 'dock' the editor so as to put it on the same window as the rest of items on the MATLAB environment. To do this, we click on the 'dock' button of the editor as illustrated in the diagram above.

Once this is done, the editor goes into the same window as the rest of items on the MATLAB environment as illustrated below.

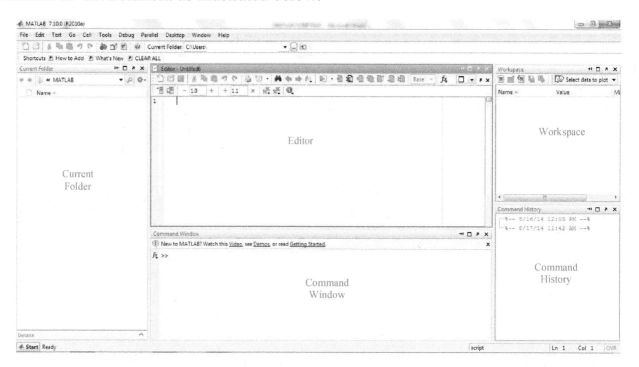

The rest of items in the MATLAB environment were clearly explained in our introductory book 'Introduction to MATLAB', our business and focus in this book is on the Editor.

NOTE: Once the Editor is docked for the first time, it does not need to be docked again, subsequent openings of the Editor will be automatically docked.

In order not to disorganize the appearance of the MATLAB environment, it is advisable to always close the software using the topmost close button as illustrated below, and not through the individual close buttons.

But if you peradventure use any of the wrong close buttons, this does not stop MATLAB from running correctly, it only keeps the window to which the close button belongs closed until you restore it.

If you know the name of the window you mistakenly closed, you can restore it by going to 'Desktop' on the MATLAB toolbar. Look for the name of the window on the drop-down menu that appears and then check it. You will usually see a list of windows on the drop-down menu, the ones that are open are checked while the ones that are closed are not checked. For instance, in our illustration in the diagram below, 6 windows are open, namely, command window, command history, current folder, workspace, editor, and titles.

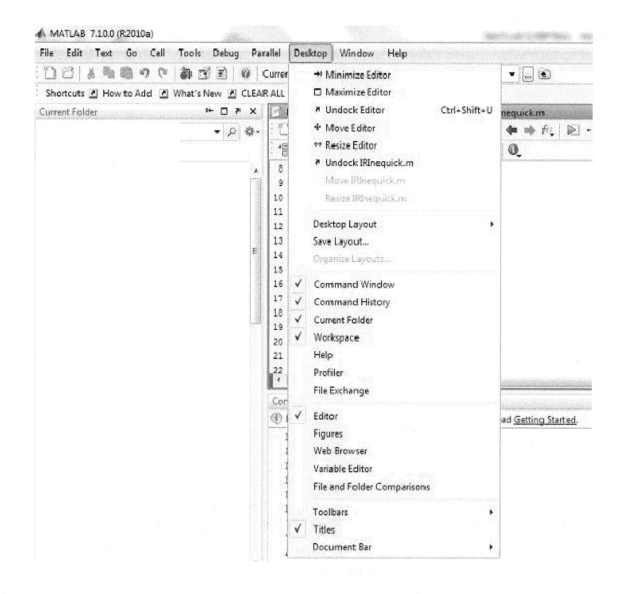

Also if for any reason your MATLAB environment gets disorganized, you can always restore it to the default MATLAB settings by also going to 'Desktop' on the MATLAB toolbar, then 'Desktop Layout', and then 'Default' as illustrated in the diagram below.

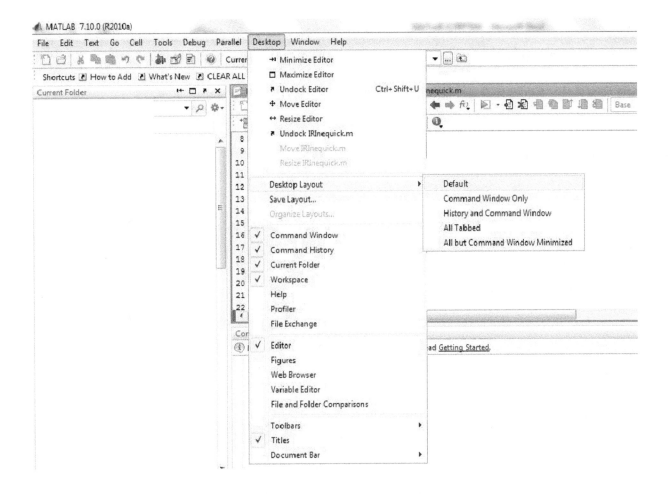

1.2 A Sample Script

As explained earlier, to develop a MATLAB script, we need to enter the series of commands to be executed by the script on the editor. Let's start with something; suppose we want a script that will do the following:

a. Construct a row vector of integers from 1 to 8

b. Transpose the row vector constructed above into a column vector

c. Construct a column vector of 8 elements and fives everywhere

d. Horizontally concatenate (join side-by-side) the column vectors of steps b and c above

We will need the following commands for each of the steps above.

Step a. To construct a row vector of integers from 1 to 8

The command is: a=1:8

And the result is: a= 1 2 3 4 5 6 7 8

Step b. To transpose the row vector constructed above into a column vector

The command is: b=a'

The result is: b =   1
                      2
                      3
                      4
                      5
                      6
                      7
                      8

Step c. To construct a column vector of 8 elements and fives everywhere

The command is: c=ones(8,1)*5

And the result is: c = 5
                        5
                        5
                        5
                        5
                        5
                        5
                        5

Step d. To horizontally concatenate (join side-by-side) the column vectors of steps b and c above

The command is: d=[b c]

Or alternatively: d=horzcat(b,c)

And the result for either command is: d =

1	5
2	5
3	5
4	5
5	5
6	5
7	5
8	5

On the editor, the 4 commands will be entered as follows:

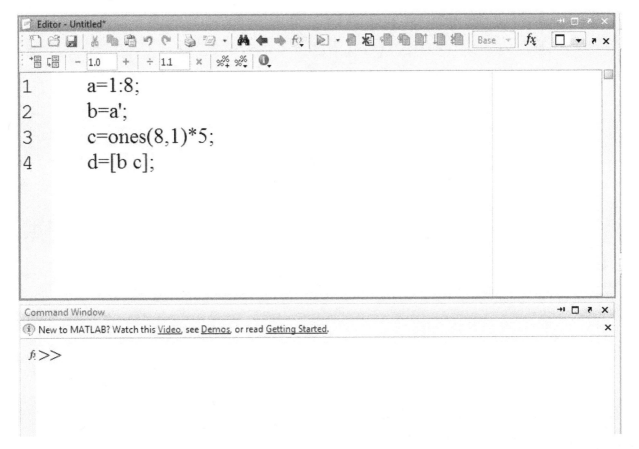

Observe the semicolon (;) at the end of each command, this is just to suppress the outputs of those commands. If we would like to see the outputs of any of the commands, then we just remove/exclude the semicolon there.

Next we need to save the script as a file so that it can be stored somewhere on our computer and we can use it from there at anytime. Saving the script is done as in most other computer program; click the save icon (illustrated below).

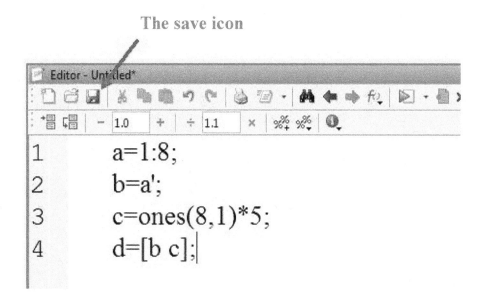

The save dialog box shows up as illustrated below. Select the folder where you want to save the script, and give it a filename of your choice (no spaces please), then click on the save button.

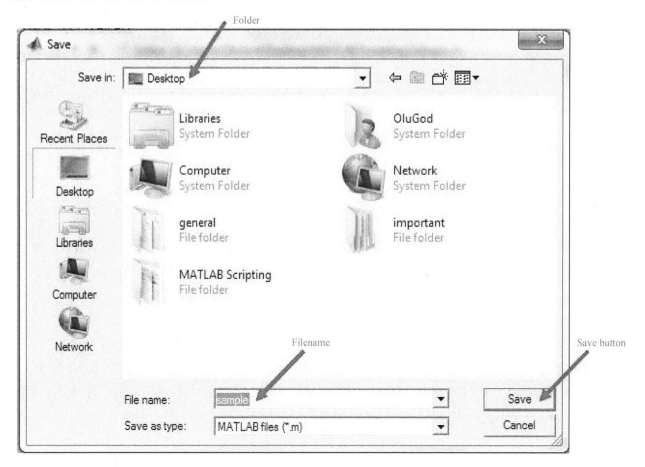

In the above illustration, we have selected to save the script on 'Desktop', and with the filename 'sample'. All MATLAB scripts are automatically saved with the file extension '.m' or '.mat'.

Once saved, you now have a MATLAB script you can run anytime, and whenever you run the script, all the commands in the script are executed sequentially starting from the first to the last, even if you have thousands of commands on the script. This is the beauty of scripting!

There is going to be enormous use of scripts in the rest of our works, so we dedicated this chapter to talking about them. Meanwhile, we are next going to be talking about how to read-in data from other external files, and how to write-out data to other external files. This is called file processing, and it is of very huge importance in computer programming.

Chapter Two:

FILE PROCESSING

Our concern in this chapter is to be able to read data from external files into MATLAB, and also to be able to write data from MATLAB to external files. We will start with the reading aspect.

2.1 Reading Data from Files

In our previous book, 'Introduction to MATLAB', we described how data can be manually imported into the MATLAB environment, but in this book we want to concentrate on automated import processes that use MATLAB codes to do same.

There are lots of functions in MATLAB that can be used to read data from external files. Some of them include load, dlmread, xlsread, textscan, fgetl, fread, fscanf, importdata, etc. In this book, we will illustrate use of the first five functions which are enough to do almost everything about reading data from external files.

load

Suppose we have data illustrated below in a file called 'sample.txt'

```
sample - Notepad
File  Edit  Format  View  Help
1500.000000    1000.000000    1500.000000
1500.000000    1100.000000    1500.000000
1500.000000    1000.000000    1500.000000
1300.000000     900.000000    1500.000000
1500.000000    1000.000000    1500.000000
800.000000      700.000000    1100.000000
500.000000      500.000000     500.000000
1500.000000    1100.000000    1500.000000
1500.000000    1000.000000    1500.000000
900.000000      700.000000    1000.000000
700.000000      700.000000     800.000000
600.000000      600.000000     600.000000
900.000000      800.000000    1100.000000
900.000000      700.000000    1000.000000
1500.000000    1000.000000    1500.000000
1500.000000     900.000000    1500.000000
1100.000000     800.000000    1500.000000
1200.000000     800.000000    1400.000000
1500.000000    1000.000000    1500.000000
1500.000000     900.000000    1500.000000
1500.000000    1100.000000    1500.000000
1500.000000    1100.000000    1500.000000
1500.000000    1200.000000    1500.000000
1500.000000    1200.000000    1500.000000
1500.000000    1200.000000    1500.000000
1400.000000     900.000000    1500.000000
900.000000      800.000000    1100.000000
900.000000      800.000000    1100.000000
800.000000      700.000000     900.000000
900.000000      800.000000    1100.000000
1500.000000     900.000000    1500.000000
900.000000      700.000000    1000.000000
800.000000      700.000000     900.000000
600.000000      500.000000     600.000000
```

We can read this data into MATLAB by simply using the command:

load('sample.txt')

And we can actually replace 'sample.txt' with whatever is the name of the file we want to read.

If we want MATLAB to recognize this data with a variable name (say, data1), then we'll say:

data1= load('sample.txt')

Then data1 will be a 3-column matrix holding the data that is contained in the file.

Note that in this illustration and the rest of this book, the data file should be kept in the same folder (or directory) as the MATLAB current folder which we illustrated in our earlier book 'Introduction to MATLAB'. Asides that, you will need to also specify the folder where the file is saved, for example: C:\Users\Daniel\Desktop\sample.txt

dlmread

In a manner that is very similar to using the load function, we can use the dlmread function to read data from external files. Suppose we wish to use the dlmread function to read data from the same file named 'sample.txt' as above, we'll simply say:

dlmread('sample.txt')

And if we need to assign this data a variable name (say, data2), then we'll use:

data2= dlmread('sample.txt')

It is important to emphasize that the load and dlmread functions can mainly be used to read in numeric data. If we have data in a file that is a mixture of texts (words or letters of the alphabet), then the next 3 functions we want to treat will be more appropriate.

xlsread

The xlsread function is designed for reading data from Microsoft Excel files.

Suppose we have data in an excel file (named 'sample.xlsx') as illustrated below:

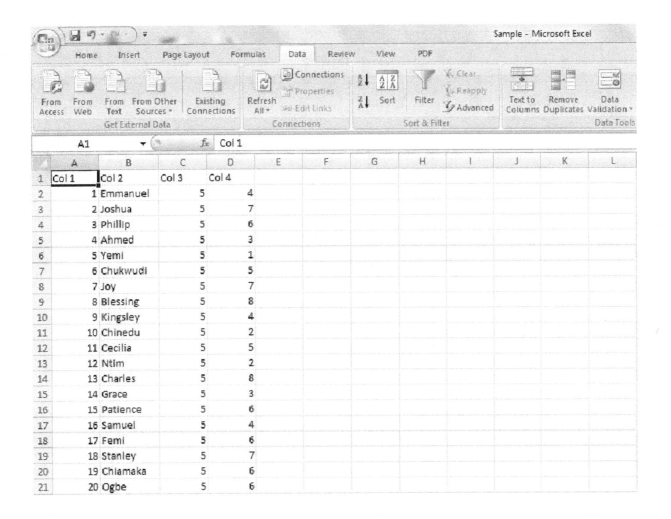

The MATLAB xlsread function can be used to read in the data into the MATLAB environment as follows:

[num, txt, raw] = xlsread('sample.xlsx')

This will read in the data as follows:
num contains all numeric data in the file
txt contains all text data in the file

raw contains all data in the file (both numeric and text)

textscan

textscan can also be used to read in both numeric and text data from text files.

Now suppose we have data illustrated below in a text file named 'sample2.txt':

```
sample2 - Notepad
File  Edit  Format  View  Help
Col 1     Col 2           Col 3     Col 4
1         Emmanuel        5         4
2         Joshua          5         7
3         Phillip         5         6
4         Ahmed           5         3
5         Yemi            5         1
6         Chukwudi        5         5
7         Joy             5         7
8         Blessing        5         8
9         Kingsley        5         4
10        Chinedu         5         2
11        Cecilia         5         5
12        Ntim            5         2
13        Charles         5         8
14        Grace           5         3
15        Patience        5         6
16        Samuel          5         4
17        Femi            5         6
18        Stanley         5         7
19        Chiamaka        5         6
20        Ogbe            5         6
21        Emeka           5         4
22        Nkechi          5         5
23        Doro            5         9
24        Kehinde         5         8
25        Adline          5         8
26        Sophia          5         5
27        Clark           5         5
28        Mustapha        5         1
29        Bello           5         1
```

Then we can read in the data column-by-column using the textscan function, but before it, we should open the file using the fopen command as follows:

fid=fopen('sample2.txt')

This opens the file named 'sample2.txt' and identifies it as 'fid' (Note that 'fid' is a variable name which can also be any name you decide to use). If the file is successfully opened, the variable 'fid' is assigned a positive integer usually greater than 3, else it is assigned a negative integer.

Next, we use textscan as below to read in the data:

data=textscan(fid, '%f %s %f %f')

But our data file carries a header line which is not part of the real data. That is this line on top of the file:

Col 1   Col 2   Col 3   Col 4

We need to indicate this as below; else the program will report an error or inadvertently do the wrong thing.

data=textscan(fid, '%f %s %f %f', 'headerlines', 1)

You could have more than 1 header line on your data file, just be sure to indicate the appropriate number as your case maybe.

That OK! But what is this junk '%f %s %f %f'?

Very important! It is the format of the data. It specifies the kind and arrangement of data in the file. The first '%f' for instance specifies that the first column of the data contains floating-point numbers, while the next '%s' says that the second column contains strings. The last two '%f %f' say that the third and fourth columns are floating-point numbers. **There is a general practice to use '%f' for numerical columns and '%s' for string (or character) columns.** So you should be able to specify the format of data in your file in that manner.

fgetl

The fgetl command is used to read in data line-by-line. Suppose, for example, we still have the same data in 'sample2.txt' above. We can use the 'fgetl' function to read-in the data in that file line-by-line into MATLAB.

Just like the 'textscan' function, we also need to first open the file using 'fopen' before we read in the data using 'fgetl'. So to proceed, we first do:

fid=fopen('sample2.txt')

and be sure 'fid' is positive, an indication that the file was successfully opened.

Then read in the first line of that file using:

ln1=fgetl(fid)

This will return the first line of that file as ln1, that is:

ln1 = Col 1   Col 2   Col 3   Col 4

Observe that 'ln1' is a variable name, and you could use any other name of your choice in its place.

Repeating the 'fgetl(fid)' command gives us the second line. That is, ln2=fgetl(fid) gives:

ln2 = 1   Emmanuel 5   4

Repeating the command again gives the third line, and so on …

In essence, we can get the first 5 lines using these set of commands:

```
fid=fopen('sample2.txt')
ln1=fgetl(fid)
ln2=fgetl(fid)
ln3=fgetl(fid)
ln4=fgetl(fid)
ln5=fgetl(fid)
```

where ln1, ln2, ln3, ln4, ln5 respectively represent the first five lines of data in the file.

But suppose we have data in several hundreds, thousands, or millions of lines, would we want to read in the data this way? That wouldn't be fair at all. Using loops will be a great way out. We will discuss how to do this in our book on 'MATLAB Loops'.

2.2 Writing Data to Files

Data processed/produced on MATLAB may often need to be written to external files to be stored for future use, especially for the case of processing lots of data. The following MATLAB functions can be used to write data to file; fprintf, xlswrite, dlmwrite, save, fwrite, etc. Knowledge of the first 2 is usually enough to accomplish data writing task, so we will only concentrate on 2 of them in this book.

fprintf

fprintf can be used to write data to text files. As with the 'textscan' function, we need to first open the file using the 'fopen' function as illustrated below. Suppose we want to write the matrix 'd' generated in chapter 1 of this book to a text file named 'output.txt', we simply do the following:

Let's first regenerate the matrix 'd' with the following commands:

```
a=1:8;
b=a';
c=ones(8,1)*;
d=[b c];
```

Then, we use fopen to open the file named 'output.txt' where the data will be written.

fid=fopen('output.txt','wt')

Notice that the 'wt' is used to indicate that this file is supposed to be 'written to' and so the program creates it if it does not already exist.

And finally we write the matrix 'd' to the file using:

fprintf(fid, '%f\t %f\n', d')

The '%f\t %f\n' here also indicates the format that the data should be written. Going with the explanation earlier given above, the format used here says that the data should be written in 2 columns (remember the matrix 'd' has 2 columns). The 'f's indicate floating-point number formats for both columns. The '\t' indicates a tab should be left between the first and second columns, and the '\n' indicates end of line after the second column so that next data is written to a new line.

The apostrophe after 'd' is used as a transpose sign to ensure the data is written correctly as the matrix 'd' should appear in MATLAB's working environment.

You will notice that the data written to 'output.txt' contains decimals. We could have done away with the decimals if we had commanded the program to write in integer formats rather than floating-point formats. To do this, we just replace the 'f's with 'd's, so that we have:

fprintf(fid, '%d\t %d\n', d')

Alternatively, we can format the output to a desired number of decimal places by doing the following as an instance.

fprintf(fid, '%2.3f\t %5.1f\n', d')

The above will format data in the first column to 2 integer places and 3 decimal places, and the data in the second column to 5 integer places and 1 decimal place.

xlswrite

xlswrite is used to write data to excel files. As an illustration, we can write the data 'd' above to an excel file named 'ouput.xlsx' by simply doing the following:

xlswrite('output.xlsx', d)

And the excel file will appear as follows:

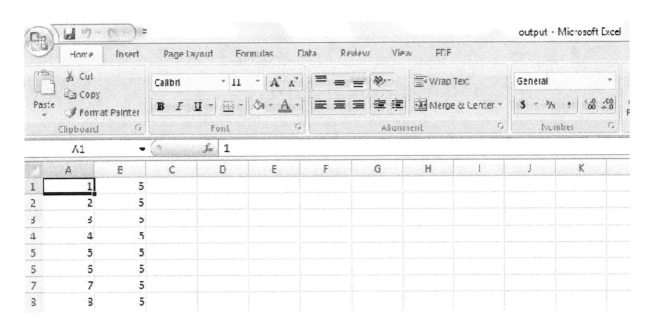

That's it! You will NOT need to use the 'fopen' function here.

Chapter Three:

INDEXING

We present a succinct treatment of indexing in this chapter since it is something we'll usually need after we read in data from file. We usually need indexing to pick particular parts of data we've read in from file for further processes in the program.

Straight to the point, if we have a matrix, say a =

4	−3	7
−6	1	11
5	20	−19
0	-27	8

We can refer to the element in row 3 and column 2 of matrix a by typing:

a(3,2)

This is called indexing, and the element there is 20 as illustrated below.

a =		
4	−3	7
−6	1	11
5	20	−19
0	-27	8

Similarly, a(4,1) will give us 0.

Practically on MATLAB, we can enter the MATRIX a as:

a=[4 -3 7; -6 1 11; 5 20 -19; 0 -27 8]

(This was explained in our earlier book on 'Introduction to MATLAB')

And now, we want you to be able to say the value of the following before you attempt them on MATLAB.

a(1,2)

a(2,1)

a(3,3)

a(2,3)

If you got -3, -6, -19, and 11 respectively, then you are very right!

Next, we can also index a set of numbers rather than just 1 number as follows: a(4,2:3)

This means the elements in row 4, columns 2 to 3. And these are [-27 8] as illustrated below.

$$
a = \begin{array}{ccc}
4 & -3 & 7 \\
-6 & 1 & 11 \\
5 & 20 & -19 \\
0 & -27 & 8
\end{array}
$$

Similarly, a(1:3,2) will give us
-3
1
20

And you should be able to say the following before attempting them on MATLAB:

a(2:4,3)

a(1,1:3)

a(1:2,2)

Answers: $\begin{matrix} 11 \\ -19 \\ 8 \end{matrix}$, [4 -3 7], and $\begin{matrix} -3 \\ 1 \end{matrix}$ respectively.

If you got that, then we take the last swipe!

We can also index an entire column or an entire row this way:

a(:,3)

This means all the rows in column 3 of matrix a (in short language, this is simply column 3 of the matrix a), and that gives: $\begin{matrix} 7 \\ 11 \\ -19 \\ 8 \end{matrix}$

Similarly, a(2,:) means the 2nd row of matrix a, and that is: [-6   1   11]

If you got that, then you sure understand what the following indexing represent:

a(4,:)

a(:,1)

Answers: [0   -27   8]   and $\begin{matrix} 4 \\ -6 \\ 5 \\ 0 \end{matrix}$ respectively.

And suppose you use an index higher than the size of the matrix, let's say a(5,:), then MATLAB will return the following error: 'Index exceeds matrix dimension'.

This is because the matrix 'a' does not have up to 5 rows. Same error will be returned for the command a(2,4), since matrix 'a' does not have up to 4 columns.

Yes! That brings us to the end of the chapter on indexing. We can now proceed to do a little project in the next chapter.

Chapter Four:

PROJECT

We put together a brief project here to test and enhance further understanding of scripting and file processing with MATLAB. Below is the project:

Develop a MATLAB script (named 'FirstProject.m' and saved in a folder named 'Folder1' anywhere on your computer). This script should do the following:

(a) Read data from an excel file named 'InitialResults.xlsx'

This excel file has only 2 columns; the first column contains student names, and the second column contains their respective exam scores (maximum score: 70).

The file is as illustrated below. You can create it and save in the same folder named 'Folder1'where the MATLAB script is also saved.

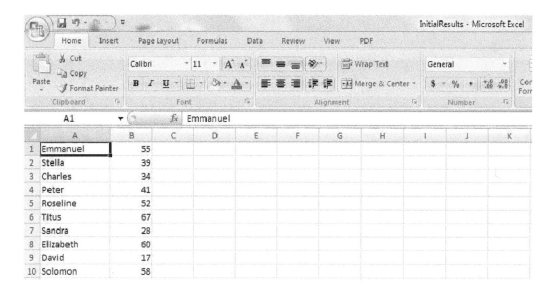

(b) The script should generate continuous assessment scores (maximum score: 30) for each student based on their exam scores. An appropriate formula to use is:

$$continuous\ assessment\ score = exam\ score \times \frac{30}{70}$$

The continuous assessment score should be rounded to the nearest integer.

(c) The script should then sum the continuous assessment and exam scores to get a total score (maximum score: 100)

(d) And finally, the script should write the output to another excel file named 'FinalResults.xsls'. The first column of this output file should have the student names, the second column should have their continuous assessment scores, the third column should have their exam scores, and the fourth column should have their total scores.

Solution:

It will be nice if you first attempt the project on your own, then pick any missing links from the solution below.

The overall code in the MATLAB script should look like something below. It doesn't have to be exactly the same since there are numerous other ways to do similar task. If your code does the task, then it is OK. We are going to take the procedure step-by-step to make sure you can follow with ease.

```
[num txt raw] = xlsread ('InitialResults.xlsx') ;
studentname=raw(:,1);
examscore=raw(:,2);
```

```
examscoreN=cell2mat(examscore);
contscore=examscoreN*30/70;
contscoreR=round(contscore);
totscore=contscoreR+examscoreN;
final(:,1)=studentname;
final(:,2)=cellstr(num2str(contscoreR));
final(:,3)=cellstr(num2str(examscoreN));
final(:,4)=cellstr(num2str(totscore));
xlswrite('FinalResults.xlsx', final);
```

Explanations:

Line 1:

```
[num txt raw]=xlsread('InitialResults.xlsx');
```

Line 1 reads in the data from the excel file named 'InitialResults.xlsx'. We need the 'raw' part of the output since we need both text (student names) and numbers (exam scores).

Lines 2 and 3:

```
studentname=raw(:,1);
examscore=raw(:,2);
```

Line 2 assigns the variable name 'studentname' to the first column of raw, while line 3 assigns the variable name 'examscore' to the second column of raw.

Line 4:

```
examscoreN=cell2mat(examscore);
```

Line 4 converts examscore from cell to matrix format, and assigns it a new variable name 'examscoreN'. We need to do this to be able to perform mathematical operations (like addition and subtraction) on the exam scores. Data from excel sheets are read-in in cell formats, and they DON'T support mathematical operations.

Line 5:

contscore=examscoreN*30/70;

Line 5 uses our earlier formula to compute the continuous assessment scores from the exam scores.

Line 6:

contscoreR=round(contscore);

Line 6 rounds the computed continuous assessment scores to the nearest integer values, and assigns them a new variable name 'contscoreR'.

Line 7:

totscore=contscoreR+examscoreN;

Line 7 sums the continuous assessment and exam scores to get the total score.

Lines 8 to 11:

final(:,1)=studentname;

final(:,2)=cellstr(num2str(contscoreR));

final(:,3)=cellstr(num2str(examscoreN));

final(:,4)=cellstr(num2str(totscore));

Line 8 places student names on column 1 of the variable name 'final', line 9 places the continuous assessment scores on column 2 of it; line 10 places the exam scores on column 3 of it; and line 11 places the total scores on column 4 of it.

Also observe that the 'num2str' and 'cellstr' functions are respectively used to convert the scores from number to string formats, and to subsequently create cell arrays from the strings.

Line 12:

xlswrite('FinalResults.xlsx', final);

Line 12 writes the final results to an excel file named 'FinalResults.xlsx'.

And that is it with the project.

If you ran your script, and got an excel file named 'FinalResults.xlsx' and looking as shown below, then you are good to go!

	A	B	C	D
1	Emmanuel	24	55	79
2	Stella	17	39	56
3	Charles	15	34	49
4	Peter	18	41	59
5	Roseline	22	52	74
6	Titus	29	67	96
7	Sandra	12	28	40
8	Elizabeth	26	60	86
9	David	7	17	24
10	Solomon	25	58	83

Next and finally, it's time to lay our hands on the problems that follow to assess how much we've learnt!

Exercises

You have data saved in a text file named 'Data.txt' as illustrated below. Use this description to answer questions in this exercise.

```
Data - Notepad
File  Edit  Format  View  Help
Hour      VTEC
0.0       15.100000
0.5       14.300000
1.0       13.600000
1.5       12.800000
2.0       11.700000
2.5       10.300000
3.0        8.760000
3.5        7.460000
4.0        6.740000
4.5        6.850000
5.0        8.000000
5.5       10.400000
6.0       14.200000
6.5       19.200000
7.0       24.500000
7.5       29.200000
8.0       32.800000
```

1. Which of the following 'textscan' commands correctly reads in all numeric data from the file after the fid=fopen('Data.txt') command has been run?

A. data=textscan(fid, '%f %f')

B. data=textscan(fid, '%f %f', 'headerlines', 1)

C. data=textscan(fid, '%f %f', 'headerlines', 2)

D. data=textscan(fid, '%s %s', 'headerlines', 1)

2. If we run the following commands on a script saved in the same folder as 'Data.txt', what strings will aa and cc respectively represent?

```
fid=fopen('Data.txt');
aa=fgetl(fid);
bb=fgetl(fid);
cc=fgetl(fid);
```

A. 'Hour VTEC' and ' 0.0   15.100000'

B. 'Hour   VTEC' and   ' 0.5   14.300000'

C. 'Hour   VTEC' and   ' 1.0   13.600000'

D. ' 0.0   15.100000'   and ' 0.5   14.300000'

3. What is the value of vtec2 if we run the following commands on a script saved in the same folder as 'Data.txt'?

```
fid=fopen('Data.txt');
data=textscan(fid,   '%f  %f',  'headerlines',  1);
data=cell2mat(data);
vtec=data(5,2);
```

A. 15.1

B. 12.8

C. 10.4

D. 11.7

4. If numeric data from that file is assigned the variable name 'data', which of the following correctly indexes the 7.46 value on that file.

A. data(3,5)

B. data(2,8)

C. data(8,2)

D. data(7,46)

5. If numeric data from that file is assigned the variable name 'data', which of the following indexing will return a MATLAB error?

A. data(10,2)

B. data(11,1)

C. data(3,1)

D. data(1,3)

6. If numeric data from that file is assigned the variable name 'data', which of the following MATLAB commands will write the data to an excel file named 'ExcelData.xlsx'?

A. xlswrite('ExcelData.xlsx')

B. dlmwrite('ExcelData.xlsx')

C. xlswrite('ExcelData.xlsx', data)

D. dlmwrite('ExcelData.xlsx', data)

7. The following commands all require the use of the 'fopen' function EXCEPT

A. dlmwrite

B. xlswrite
C.   fprintf
D. textscan

8. If you run the command 'fid=fopen('Data.txt')' and get a negative value for fid, which of the following is most likely?

A. The file contains only negative numbers

B. The file contains some negative numbers

C. The number of negative values in the file exceeds the number of positive values in it

D. The file with the exact name 'Data.txt' does not exist in the same folder from where the command is run

9. If numeric data from the file is assigned the variable name 'data', which of the following MATLAB commands will correctly write the data to a text file named 'TextData.txt'?

A. fid=fopen('TextData.txt', 'wt'); fprintf(fid, '%f\t %f\n', data');

B. fid=fopen('TextData.txt', 'wt'); fprintf(fid, '%f\t %f\t', data');

C. fid=fopen('TextData.txt', 'wt'); fprintf(fid, '%f\n %f\n', data');

D. fid=fopen('TextData.txt', 'wt'); fprintf(fid, '%f %f', data');

10. If numeric data from the file is assigned the variable name 'data', which of the following MATLAB commands will return exactly the same answer as data(1:6,1)?

A. 0:0.5:2.5

B. (0:0.5:2.5)'

C. (1:6:1)'

D. ones(1,6)

Answers

1. B

2. B

3. D

4. C

5. D

6. C

7. A

8. D

9. A

10. B

www.ingramcontent.com/pod-product-compliance
Lightning Source LLC
LaVergne TN
LVHW060149070326
832902LV00018B/3025